Worst
Natural Disasters

Karen Uhler

Series Editor
Jeffrey D. Wilhelm

Much thought, debate, and research went into choosing and ranking the 10 items in each book in this series. We realize that everyone has his or her own opinion of what is most significant, revolutionary, amazing, deadly, and so on. As you read, you may agree with our choices, or you may be surprised — and that's the way it should be!

Franklin Watts®

an imprint of

SCHOLASTIC

www.scholastic.com/librarypublishing

A Rubicon book published in association with Scholastic Inc.

Ru'bicon © 2007 Rubicon Publishing Inc.
www.rubiconpublishing.com

Associate Publishers: Kim Koh, Miriam Bardswich
Project Editor: Amy Land
Editor: Bettina Fehrenbach
Creative Director: Jennifer Drew
Project Manager/Designer: Jeanette MacLean

The publisher gratefully acknowledges the following for permission to reprint copyrighted material in this book.

Every reasonable effort has been made to trace the owners of copyrighted material and to make due acknowledgment. Any errors or omissions drawn to our attention will be gladly rectified in future editions.

"Chasing Tornadoes: More Than Just a Thrill" (excerpt), by Corey Binns. © 1999 – 2006 Imaginova Corp. October 2, 2006. Reprinted with permission.

"New Orleans Levees Not Built for Worst Case Events" (excerpt), by Brian Handwerk. From National Geographic News, September 2, 2005. Reprinted with permission.

"Miles upon miles of stinking mud: A reporter's tale of Colombian disaster begins with rescue" (excerpt), by Tomas Guillen. From the *Seattle Times*, November 24, 1985. Reprinted with permission.

"The Food Crisis in Niger" (excerpt), from National Black Catholic Congress, Inc. Article printed with the permission of the National Black Catholic Congress; visit the NBCC Web site at: www.nbccongress.org.

Cover image: A New Orleans fireman helps evacuate a man out of flood waters during the aftermath of Hurricane Katrina – © SHANNON STAPLETON/Reuters/Corbis

Library and Archives Canada Cataloguing in Publication

Uhler, Karen
    The 10 worst natural disasters / Karen Uhler.

Includes index.
ISBN 978-1-55448-469-0

    1. Readers (Elementary) 2. Readers—Natural disasters.
I. Title. II. Title: Ten worst natural disasters.

PE1117.U45 2007   428.6   C2007-900541-1

1 2 3 4 5 6 7 8 9 10   10   16 15 14 13 12 11 10 09 08 07

Printed in Singapore

Contents

6

10

22

TRAGEDY STRIKES AGAIN!

It seems as though every time we turn on the news, terrifying pictures fill the TV screen. Why? Because another natural disaster has hit! Images of destruction, heartbreaking stories of injuries and death, and powerful accounts of heroic rescues — how do you feel when you see them? Frightened and awed by the power of nature to destroy, or sad for the victims and survivors?

Natural disasters come in all varieties. Some don't cause very much damage, but others leave behind a trail of destruction that takes years to clean up. From record-setting earthquakes to deadly landslides and explosive volcanoes, you can never know when a disaster will happen.

Sure, there can be warning signs, but that doesn't necessarily mean people will evacuate or that the disaster will strike at that moment.

So how did we choose the 10 worst natural disasters? It wasn't easy. These are the criteria we used: disasters that have caused an enormous amount of damage to the area; disasters with high fatalities; disasters that have uprooted a few people to millions of people; and the costs of rebuilding cities and communities lost in the disasters. As you read, focus on these criteria and decide …

WHAT IS THE WORST NATURAL DISASTER?

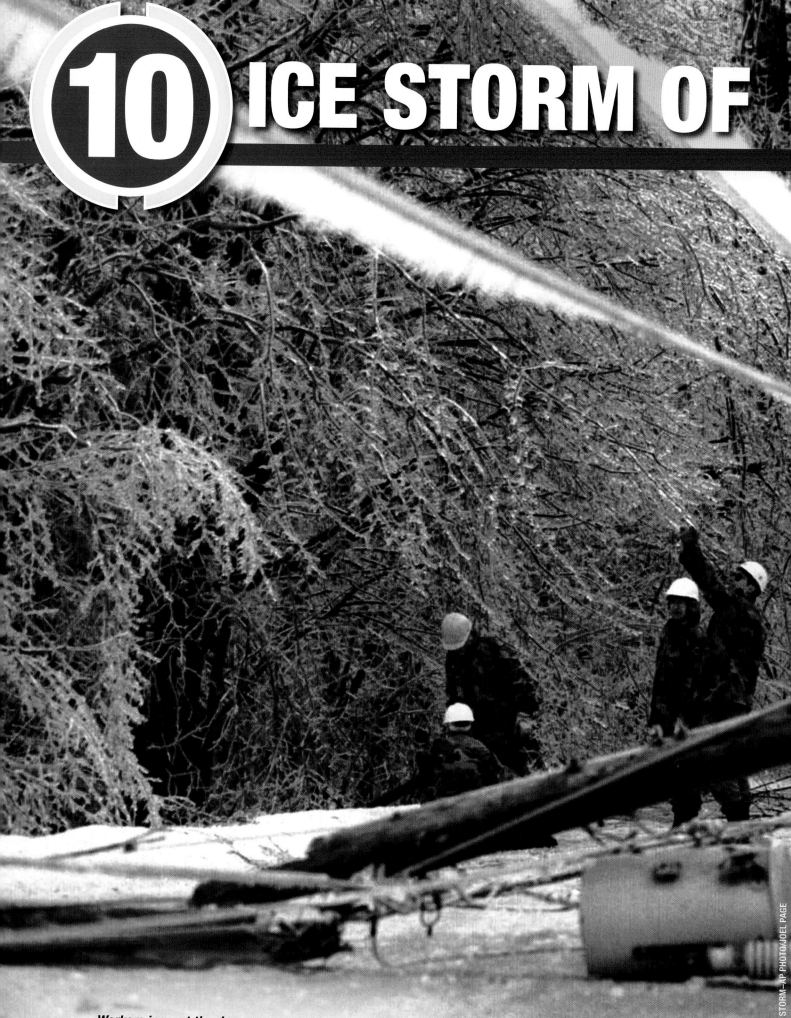

Workers inspect the damage caused by the storm.

ICE STORM—AP PHOTO/JOEL PAGE

1998

PLACE: Parts of New York, New England, and Eastern Canada

WHEN: January 5-10, 1998

LEVEL OF DESTRUCTION: Several million people were left without electricity for weeks. Many homes, businesses, and trees were destroyed.

The ice storm of 1998 created a beautiful but deadly winter tragedy. More slippery than snow, freezing rain clings to everything it touches. For over six days, the storm coated parts of New England and New York, as well as parts of the Canadian provinces of New Brunswick, Ontario, and Quebec.

Imagine losing electricity in your house (as well as heat and hot water), in the middle of a severe North American winter. Power lines were down and fallen trees blocked many roads. Everywhere you looked, freezing branches were crashing down on cars and houses. Entire cities and towns were in darkness. More than four million people were without electricity for days. Over 700,000 people were still without power three weeks after the storm!

 How would you spend your days without school and without power at home?

ICE STORM OF 1998

WHAT HAPPENED?

The 1998 ice storm dumped almost four inches of freezing rain, coating everything with layers of ice. It did not rain continuously. Instead, each episode lasted only a few hours. This allowed the rain to crystallize and add weight to anything it touched. It rained for a total of 80 hours — nearly double the normal annual total.

WHAT'S THE DAMAGE?

This icy chiller caused widespread damage to public and private properties. Over $5 million worth of damage made this the costliest natural disaster to ever hit the northeastern U.S. and Canada. The agriculture and livestock industries were the worst hit. Meat processing plants were shut down, and the milk and maple syrup industries suffered tremendous losses.

livestock: *animals raised for food*

? How would the damage to crops and livestock affect you and your family?

CASUALTIES

Lives lost: 17 people in the U.S.; 28 people in Canada

Injured/affected: More than 900 people, mostly due to hypothermia

PICKING UP THE PIECES

To clean up this storm, the U.S. government sent in thousands of National Guards to states like New York, Maine, and Vermont. These guards helped to clear roads, rescue people, and provide food and shelter for those in need. Electrical workers labored around the clock for days trying to restore power.

hypothermia: *dangerous loss of body temperature*

Quick Fact

Former Governor George Pataki's residence in New York City was one of the many homes without power.

The Expert Says...

"There's no water. There's no heat. There're no lights. There's no gas. There's nothing. It's real bad. I can't imagine how people are going to cope the longer it goes on."

— Diane Brayton, a coordinator of a Red Cross shelter in Gouverneur, New York

Quick Fact

According to one expert, the ice storm brought down enough wires and cables to stretch around the world three times.

FLASH FREEZE

Having a hard time imagining the damage done by this ice storm? Take a look at this photo essay to see the effect of this storm on cities and towns.

A worker for Asplundh Tree Service clears ice-covered branches near power lines in Watertown, N.Y. after an ice storm left a two-inch-thick coating of ice on January 9, 1998.

A minivan sits damaged by a downed utility pole.

A group of neighbors walk near a large tree limb which fell onto power lines on Rt. 202 near New Gloucester, Maine.

Take Note

The amount of ice, the length of the event, the extreme cold, and the extent of the area affected were significant in the 1998 ice storm. On top of that, it hit one of the most populated regions of North America, affecting millions of lives. It truly was the worst ice storm of modern times, earning it the #10 spot on our list.

• For those living elsewhere, the 1998 ice storm may just seem like life without electricity. Do you think those who lived through this storm felt the same way? How might they describe their experiences to let others know what the storm was like?

(9) TORNADO OUT

Three tornadoes make their way through a midwestern state.

BREAK OF 1974

PLACE: Southeast and Midwest United States

WHEN: April 3–4, 1974

LEVEL OF DESTRUCTION: This horrific once-in-a-millennium event showed us the unbelievable raw power of nature. The path of destruction killed hundreds and destroyed a large part of the United States.

If you thought one tornado was bad enough, then imagine 148 of them twisting across 13 states. This disaster became known as the Super Tornado Outbreak of 1974. It was the worst outbreak of tornadoes in North America. At its peak, there were 15 tornadoes on the ground at the same time. In less than 18 hours, 315 people were killed, 6,000 were injured, and 888 square miles of countryside were destroyed.

This wasn't just a bit of windy weather. Some of these twisters had wind speeds of over 300 mph! Trees were ripped from the ground and houses were pulled from their foundations. Cars and trucks were carried more than 164 feet. One eyewitness said, "It looked like an angry boy had thrown his toys."

TORNADO OUTBREAK OF 1974

WHAT HAPPENED?

This number of tornadoes in such a short time seems like something that could only happen in a terrifying disaster movie. A tornado's intensity is rated using the Fujita scale, which goes from F0 (light winds) to F5 (incredible damage). Of the 148 tornadoes, six were F5s with winds clocking in at over 300 mph — that's strong enough to lift and carry a house! The worst F5 destroyed the town of Xenia, Ohio. In all, there were 24 F4s with winds ranging from 205 to 258 mph.

What would you do if you knew a tornado was heading for your town and home?

WHAT'S THE DAMAGE?

More than 27,000 homes and buildings were damaged. Total economic damage was estimated at $600 million. The worst states hit during this disaster were Kentucky, Tennessee, Indiana, Illinois, Ohio, Alabama, and Georgia.

Where do you think is the safest place to be during a tornado?

CASUALTIES

Lives lost: 330
Injured/affected: 6,000

PICKING UP THE PIECES

Most of the relief for this disaster came from local groups such as churches and small businesses. The Red Cross was the biggest agency to help out, finding shelter for many of the homeless. Women's groups prepared meals for those in need. Donations of clothing were sent from across the country.

The Expert Says...

"As devastating as that day was, we did learn a lot. We learned about storm movement. We learned about tornado formation and actions. And we learned a lot about our agency and how well we were able to function to keep people safe from harm.

— Richard P. Augulis, director of the Weather Service Central Region

Quick Fact

Tornadoes form during thunderstorms — warm moist air rises, cools, and condenses, forming rain. This downdraft of rain meets winds of a different speed closer to the ground and the spinning begins. But tornadoes don't always form, making them difficult to predict.

TORNADO HUNTERS

An article from Live Science, MSNBC
By Corey Binns, October 2, 2006

They may sound like daredevils, but storm watchers help improve forecasts

People who hunt down tornadoes sometimes get a bad rap as reckless, thrill-seeking daredevils. Most of the time, the reality is a lot less exciting than the dramatic photos and a few seconds of video suggest. Tornado hunters spend most of their time driving around, eating fast food, and sleeping in cramped quarters.

"It's thrilling," said storm chaser and Purdue University meteorologist Robert Jeff Trapp. "But it's not glamorous. ... It can be disappointing. The times we've been successful have been incredible experiences."

There are two types of tornado aficionados who will endure the boredom for the suspense of a storm: spotters and chasers. ...

Today, storm spotters are all volunteers, trained by the National Weather Service's SkyWarn program to know what to look for and, if they see something, what to do. ... Storm chasers, on the other hand, work to gather more intensive data that is used over the longer term to continue improving the science of forecasts. ...

With the help of chasers, their cameras, and some modern mobile instruments, scientists are trying to learn more about how tornadoes form. ...

So what drives these chasers? "The challenge aspect is always a lot of fun," Trapp said. "There's a camaraderie, too. Typically after a big storm day, there'll be a chance gathering at a local restaurant. We swap stories and video. It's fun to hear other people's stories. It takes a different kind of person to be patient and drive around for all of that time. They tend to appreciate nature."

aficionados: fans, enthusiasts
camaraderie: friendship; companionship

Quick Fact

Maybe some good did come from this disaster. Studying the outbreak helped engineers learn the best ways to protect people in buildings during severe weather.

Take Note

Tornadoes can be scary things, especially because they're so unpredictable. This 1974 incident was the worst tornado outbreak in recorded history. It is ranked #9 because many areas and lives were affected.
- Imagine losing your home and everything in it to a tornado. What would you miss the most?

Residents of New Orleans try to escape the floods.

KATRINA

PLACE: Alabama, Florida, Mississippi, and Louisiana

WHEN: Late August, 2005

LEVEL OF DESTRUCTION: This was the costliest natural disaster in U.S. history. Almost 2,000 people lost their lives and thousands were left homeless.

Imagine winds strong enough to blow the roof off your house. Imagine people stranded on their roofs for days because that was the only place to escape the floods. Imagine fires, looting, and bodies floating in the streets. Then imagine a sports dome filled to capacity with thousands upon thousands of scared and angry people whose homes have been destroyed.

Hurricane Katrina devastated most of the U.S. Gulf Coast. The city of New Orleans, Louisiana, experienced catastrophic damage. Some neighborhoods were under as much as 20 feet of water.

Katrina got its name when it first formed over the Bahamas on August 23, 2005. It was the 11th storm of the season. Despite warnings from the government, many people were unable to evacuate because they didn't have transportation. They just hoped that the hurricane would not hit land.

Turn the page to find out more about one of the strongest hurricanes to hit U.S. soil …

catastrophic: *relating to a great and sudden disaster*

HURRICANE KATRINA

WHAT HAPPENED?

Katrina started out as a weak category 1 hurricane. By August 27, it had picked up enough energy from the Gulf of Mexico to reach a category 5 status with winds of over 174 mph. Even though it was downgraded to a category 3 hurricane, the wind speed was still over 99 mph when it hit the southern states. Katrina dumped rain at a rate of almost an inch per hour.

WHAT'S THE DAMAGE?

The damage from Katrina added up to over $80 billion! The states of Alabama, Mississippi, and Louisiana were hit the hardest. Cities like Biloxi, Gulf Port, Mobile, and Waveland were badly damaged, but the story of Katrina's wrath centered on New Orleans. Most of New Orleans is below sea level so it needs levees to prevent flooding. Hurricane Katrina caused these levees to collapse and millions of gallons of water flowed into the city, filling it like a cereal bowl. The sad fact is that these levees were unable to withstand the fury of Katrina.

---

levees: *structures that prevent flooding*

 Research why the levees were unable to withstand the fury of Katrina.

CASUALTIES

Lives lost: More than 1,800
Injured/affected: Thousands of people lost their homes and over three million were without electricity for months.

PICKING UP THE PIECES

There was a worldwide response to this disaster. More than 70 countries pledged donations of money or other forms of assistance. Kuwait donated the most — $500 million. Qatar gave $100 million. India and China both donated $5 million. Other countries, including Canada, Mexico, Singapore, and Germany, sent aid in the form of supplies, relief personnel, troops, ships, and water pumps.

This is an aerial view of houses in New Orleans swamped by floodwaters after Hurricane Katrina.

The Expert Says...

"We were seeing the laws of chance operating there. Katrina was near maximum intensity when it hit landfall and it hit a very vulnerable place."

— Kerry Emanuel, professor of meteorology in the MIT Department of Earth, Atmospheric, and Planetary Sciences

Quick Fact

Hurricanes are given male and female names because they are easier to remember than confusing latitude and longitude directions. The name Katrina has been retired because the 2005 storm was so deadly.

New Orleans Levees Not Built for Worst Case Events

An article from *National Geographic News*
By Brian Handwerk, September 2, 2005

New Orleans is surrounded by water — Lake Pontchartrain, the Mississippi River, and the nearby Gulf of Mexico. Resting an average of six feet below sea level, the city's safety has long depended on one of the world's most extensive levee systems. ...

The bowl-like shape of New Orleans prevents water from draining away, as broken levees continue to allow water to flow into city streets. No one is sure how long it will take to pump out floodwaters once the levees are repaired.

Lt. Gen. Carl Strock, chief of engineers for the Corps, dismissed suggestions that recent federal funding decreases or delayed contracts had any impact on levee performance in the face of Katrina's overwhelming force.

Instead he pointed to a danger that many public officials had warned about for years: The system was never designed to withstand a storm of Katrina's strength.

"We were just caught by a storm whose intensity exceeded the protection that we had in place."

... [D]etermining the level of protection needed versus what Congress and the public are willing to pay for isn't often easy.

Acceptable risks must be weighed, including the statistical likelihood of catastrophic events and the possible consequences if they do occur, according to U.S. Army Corps of Engineers officials. ...

The current system in New Orleans was designed decades ago and has been shaped over time by past storms.

An unnamed hurricane on September 1947 flooded Jefferson Parish, which includes metropolitan New Orleans, to depths of about three feet. The storm caused 100 million dollars worth of damage.

New Orleans fire rescue worker helps a family who spent 10 hours in an attic

After the storm, hurricane protection levees were built along Lake Pontchartrain's south shore.

Hurricane Betsy made landfall some 50 miles east of New Orleans on September 10, 1965. Winds in the city reached 125 miles per hour and the storm surge neared 10 feet. After extensive flooding, the Orleans Levee Board raised existing levees to a height of 12 feet. ...

Still, traffic snarls illustrated the difficulty and danger that would accompany evacuation in the face of a more direct hit — like the one delivered by Hurricane Katrina.

Take Note

Within a matter of days, Katrina wreaked havoc and made an entire region appear like a war zone. The lives lost and property damage were significantly larger. Their economic and political outcomes still linger today. Hurricane Katrina earned our #8 ranking for being, by far, a more devastating natural disaster.

- Do you think the Katrina disaster will influence governments and people to better prepare for the next hurricane? What course of action would you suggest?

At 22,205 feet above sea level, Mount Huascarán is the highest mountain in Peru.

MOUNT HUASCARAN—© RICHARD LIST/CORBIS

YUNGAY, PERU

PLACE: Yungay (Jun-guy), Peru, a town near the base of Mount Huascarán [Was'ka-ran]

WHEN: May 31, 1970

LEVEL OF DESTRUCTION: A white blanket of death completely destroyed a whole town, almost wiping out its entire population.

From the small town of Yungay, people could admire the highest peak in Peru — the awesome snow-capped Mount Huascarán. However, on May 31, 1970, nature delivered a one-two punch — an earthquake that triggered a catastrophic avalanche. The earthquake lasted only 45 seconds, but it was so strong that it shook Mount Huascarán, starting an avalanche that sent snow, rocks, and debris sliding down the mountain. This rolling, tumbling blanket of ice, rock, and snow covered the town completely, destroying it and the people who lived there.

The earthquake that caused this avalanche affected other towns in Peru and destroyed communication, commerce, and transportation around Yungay. Roads were ruined, and people couldn't get in or out of the towns. Parts of Peru came to a standstill.

AVALANCHE
IN YUNGAY, PERU

WHAT HAPPENED?

The earthquake that triggered this avalanche measured a strong 7.9 on the Richter scale. The tremors and shock waves sent a huge slab of snow, ice, mud, and rubble tumbling down Mount Huascarán. But this wasn't any run-of-the-mill avalanche. It was estimated that the ice slab was 2,953 feet wide and almost a mile long. It tumbled down the mountain at speeds of almost 100 mph.

WHAT'S THE DAMAGE?

Not only was Yungay buried by the avalanche, but the shock of the earthquake destroyed many homes, factories, and schools. Electricity, water, and sanitary and communications facilities in the region were also damaged. This damage seriously weakened relief efforts. It is estimated that economic losses were over $500 million!

> **?** How do you think the lives of the survivors changed?

Richter scale: *system used to rank the strength of an earthquake; for instance, a 7.0 is 10x more powerful than a 6.0, and 100x more powerful than a 5.0*

Quick Fact

An avalanche is also referred to as "White Death."

CASUALTIES

Lives lost: 20,000 were killed by the avalanche

Injured/affected: 400 townspeople survived but had to be resettled.

PICKING UP THE PIECES

Two Peruvian Air Force planes carried relief supplies to the area and troops were sent to open up roads to areas cut off by the avalanche. The United Nations offered to provide technical assistance and aid, but there were few survivors. The Peruvian government has forbidden excavation, or digging, in the area where the town of Yungay is buried, declaring it a national cemetery. Yungay was left as a ruin and became a sightseeing stop for tourists.

> **?** Do you think it's right that Yungay is now a tourist site? Why or why not?

The Expert Says...

In the face of such disaster, there is a feeling of admiration for the people who survived. …
I could not shake the feeling that I was walking on top of a whole town. … It was haunting.

— Corine J. Quarterman, an excerpt from "Huarascarán National Park, Peru" in the book *Odyssey: A Woman's Global Adventures*

A CITY DESTROYED

BEFORE

YUNGAY ANTES

These photos show what Yungay looked like before and after the avalanche. The city and its 20,000 inhabitants were buried beneath approximately 80 million cubic yards of mud and rubble. There is now a memorial park on the site of the disaster.

AQUI ESTUVO YUNGAY
(25,000 habitantes)

PLAZA DE ARMAS

AFTER

Quick Fact

The earthquake of 1970 that initially set off the avalanche also devastated other areas of Peru, killing close to 50,000 people.

Take Note

The ice storm of 1998 and Hurricane Katrina caused heavy damage and loss of lives. However, they do not stack up against the massive loss of lives in the Yungay avalanche. This worst avalanche on record earns our #7 ranking.

• Have you ever experienced any of the disasters described so far? Do you feel lucky or safe to live where you do? Explain your answer.

Aerial view of the town of Armero, dated November 18, 1985, after the Nevado del Ruiz volcano erupted. It spewed rocks, water, mud, and ash over sleeping towns.

PLACE: Armero, Colombia, a village at the base of Nevado del Ruiz in the Andes mountains

WHEN: November 13, 1985

LEVEL OF DESTRUCTION: Colombia's highest active volcano erupted. As the volcanic flow moved down the mountain, it mixed with mud and completely destroyed several towns. Over 22,000 were killed.

This disaster at Colombia shares a lot of similarities with the disaster you just read about at #7. They both take place in South America in the Andes mountains. They both involve small towns covered with debris that slid off a mountain. But Nevado del Ruiz wasn't shaken by an earthquake — the disaster was caused by an active volcano.

The big difference between this and Yungay is that this tragedy could have been avoided. Nevado del Ruiz had given off warning signs — a steady stream of small earthquakes for over two years before the disaster struck. This volcanic activity was enough to make people nervous, but not enough to scare them away. They didn't truly believe the volcano would erupt and destroy their town. This is understandable because people don't like to leave their homes. In addition, authorities weren't evacuating the residents, so they stayed put. Although the final eruption wasn't huge, the landslide it triggered was deadly.

? Would you evacuate your home if you knew the volcano looming over your town could erupt? Why or why not?

LANDSLIDE
IN NEVADO DEL RUIZ, COLOMBIA

WHAT HAPPENED?

The Nevado del Ruiz volcano was known as "the sleeping lion," but on November 13, 1985, this lion roared. The ash from the eruption mixed with the water from melting snow to create volcanic mud flow known as a lahar. A Lahar is just like wet concrete. It flows down the mountain and becomes rock hard when dry. By 1:00 AM on November 14, the flow had stopped, but Armero was left buried in over 16 feet of mud and debris.

WHAT'S THE DAMAGE?

Relief and resettlement of thousands of displaced residents cost the Colombian government $7.7 billion. But it was the human death toll that makes it the second worst volcanic eruption of the 20th century. It is perhaps the most disastrous landslide in modern times.

CASUALTIES

Lives lost: More than 22,000
Injured/affected: 4,500 people injured, 8,000 left homeless

Quick Fact

Fifteen thousand animals also died in this disaster.

PICKING UP THE PIECES

After this disaster struck, the Red Cross and the United Nations Department of Humanitarian Affairs came in to help out. Along with cash donations, the government requested items like tents, blankets, clothing, medicine, and food. Organizations including World Vision, Oxfam, and UNICEF all donated supplies. The Volcano Disaster Assistance Program (VDAP) was launched to better respond to and prevent such a disaster in the future.

? What are the benefits of other countries offering to help with relief efforts after a natural disaster?

The Expert Says...

"Within hours, people were dead or missing in a mile-wide avalanche of ash and mud. Thousands more were injured, orphaned, and homeless. The Colombian town of Armero had virtually disappeared.

— George Russell, *TIME* magazine

Quick Fact

Even into the 1990s, Armero was still covered in a massive amount of debris. Local villagers were still finding human bones belonging to victims who lost their lives during this tragedy.

10   9   8   7   6

A Volcano's Toll: Disaster in Colombia

An article from *The Seattle Times*
By Tomas Guillen, November 24, 1985

… Driving in the dark from Mariquita, to the village of Guayabal, then toward Armero, we could smell the disaster before we saw it. There was the mud, and there was the smell of decay of thousands of animal and human bodies.

In first light we could see the devastation. …

A cow, neck-deep in the ooze, mooed mournfully in the eerie morning, but mostly there was silence. In some places, telephone poles showed how deep the mud had flowed; it rose almost to their crossbars. In other places it was impossible to tell the depth.

Up the road we met a driver who had been waiting for light, to drive his gasoline tanker into the area to refuel emergency vehicles. Urgently, he pointed to where the flowing mud had parted to create an island of brush and trees. There was a farmhouse and several smaller

A Colombian soldier and rescue worker evacuate an injured woman following the eruption of the Nevado Del Ruiz Volcano, November 13, 1985

buildings. The driver said, "Una nina llora! (A little girl cries). Mira (Look). Mija grita, llore! (Little girl, cry!)"

The high-pitched voice cried out from somewhere within the island, across a 40-yard-wide channel of mud. We couldn't pinpoint the voice, and we didn't want to go into the mud. …

The mud roared like ten thousand bulls running wild, survivors said. It swept away whole families. It caught fleeing victims just feet outside their homes. It leveled the town. …

To survive such a battering was a miracle, and the deaths vastly outnumbered the miracles. …

Quick Fact

Before the disaster, Armero was known as the "White City" because of all of its rice and cotton fields.

Take Note

The fact that this tragedy could have been avoided places this disaster on our list at #6. Because of the greater number of lives lost, we've ranked this landslide higher than the avalanche.
• Why do you think people choose to live in such dangerous places?

5   4   3   2   1

5 MOUNT PELÉE

Two men walk through rubble-filled roads in the town of Saint-Pierre.

RUBBLE-FILLED STREETS—© CORBIS

ERUPTION

PLACE: Saint-Pierre on the Caribbean island of Martinique

WHEN: May 8, 1902

LEVEL OF DESTRUCTION: Very hot gas, steam, and ash swept down the mountain at speeds of 99 mph! It destroyed an entire city and the people who lived there.

Close your eyes and visualize lush vegetation, a warm inviting climate, palm trees swaying in a light breeze, and a beautiful view of a mountain. Sadly, this mountain held a deadly secret.

In May of 1902, Mount Pelée exploded, destroying the city of Saint-Pierre and killing all but a few of its residents. The destructive force of this awesome eruption was not lava, but a cloud of superheated gas, steam, and glowing ash.

What makes this disaster worse is that the governor of the town was up for re-election. He told the newspapers to write about how the volcano would not erupt and how safe everyone was. This way, the townspeople would stay and vote for him.

 How do you feel about this governor who put the lives of his townspeople in danger?

Saint-Pierre was once a vibrant, colonial city known to Europeans as the "Paris of the West Indies." It was known for its beauty, but it would soon be demolished by Mount Pelée. This eruption is known as the worst volcanic disaster of the 20th century.

MOUNT PÉLÉE ERUPTION

Quick Fact
Earth's crust is made up of 15 plates that are always moving. They float on top of very hot liquid rock (called magma). When pressure builds up between two plates, magma is forced up to the surface, causing volcanic eruptions.

WHAT HAPPENED?

Mount Pelée, an active volcano, started rumbling and grumbling in late April of 1902, sending smoke and ash up into the air. A month later, on May 8, Mount Pelée erupted. Deadly pyroclastic flows rolled down the mountain at an estimated speed of 99 miles per hour. This hot cloud had temperatures higher than 2,358°F — enough to instantly kill humans and animals.

pyroclastic flows: *very hot gas, steam, and ash formed during an eruption*

WHAT'S THE DAMAGE?

The volcano demolished the entire city of Saint-Pierre. Surrounding towns were also affected because Saint-Pierre was the economic center of the island of Martinique. At the beginning of the 20th century, it was the most modern town in the Caribbean. Saint-Pierre had electricity and telephones, and attracted many tourists. The volcano was powerful enough to destroy 20 ships in the harbor.

Would you be willing to move to an area with a volcano looming over your town? Why or why not?

CASUALTIES

Lives lost: 28,000
Injured/affected: Two residents survived.

PICKING UP THE PIECES

The two remaining survivors were resettled, but nothing could be done to save this once-modern city. Years after the disaster, a new city was rebuilt on the dried ash and lava that had destroyed Saint-Pierre.

A man sitting on Orange Hill surveys the ruins of the town of Saint-Pierre.

Over the last 5,000 years, Mount Pelée has erupted more than 30 times!

Quick Fact
The word volcano comes from the Latin name *vulcanus*, which means "all mountains that give off smoke and fire." In Roman mythology, Vulcan was the god of fire.

The Expert Says...

" In 1902, the population of Martinique ignored the dangers posed by such an explosive volcano, and didn't realize that the city of Saint-Pierre was exposed to the consequences of the ongoing eruption. "

— Thierry Lesales, Ph.D., geographer

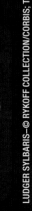

PRETTY DARN LUCKY

Amazingly, only two people survived Mount Pelée's explosive eruption. Check out the survivors' profiles and miraculous stories!

THE PRISONER
Ludger Sylbaris (also known as Louis-Auguste Cyparis)

Ludger's punishment ended up saving his life! He was locked up in the city jail in a very solid cell with only one small opening. On the day of the eruption, he said it got very dark. Then very hot air and ash entered the opening of his cell. Although the heat lasted a short time, he was very badly burned. When his burns healed, he was pardoned. He then joined the circus as "the man who lived through doomsday."

pardoned: officially forgiven for an offense

THE SHOEMAKER
The Shoemaker – Léon Compere-Léandre

It is believed that Léon survived because his house was a bit farther away from the path of the pyroclastic flow. Even though he was badly burned, he was able to run to the next town. He described what had happened: "I felt a terrible wind blowing, the earth began to tremble, and the sky suddenly became dark. I turned to go into the house ... and felt my arms and legs burning, also my body. ... At this moment four others sought refuge in my room, crying and writhing with pain. ... I got up and went to another room, where I found the father Delavaud, still clothed and lying on the bed, dead. He was purple and inflated, but the clothing was intact. ..."

Ludger Sylbaris shows the scars left from his burns.

Take Note

During the Mount Pelée eruption of 1902, the town governor's lies led to a devastating loss of lives. This, and the speed at which the volcano killed, earned its place at #5 on our list.

- Saint-Pierre has since been rebuilt and attracts tourists from all over the world. If you were visiting this city, what would you want to know about it and what would you want to see? Why?

4 EARTHQUAKE

Sometimes Earth's plates get squeezed or pushed against one another and get stuck. Eventually they are released, and all the energy that has built up causes an earthquake.

IN CHILE

PLACE: Pacific Ocean, roughly 99 miles off the west coast of Chile, South America

WHEN: May 22, 1960

LEVEL OF DESTRUCTION: This massive quake was the largest ever recorded. It didn't just destroy several towns and villages — it had the power to change Earth's surface.

Imagine: the ground you are standing on shakes you enough to knock you off your feet. These kinds of rumblings from deep beneath Earth's surface can be scary and deadly. Now imagine an earthquake so monstrous that it changes the landscape of a country forever.

An earthquake as powerful as the one in Chile only happens about once every 20 years. The strength of an earthquake is measured by the Richter scale. The weakest an earthquake can be is 0.1 on the scale. Most earthquakes are less than 2.5, and these are barely felt. With each rise in number, the earthquake is 10 times stronger. This earthquake was 9.5 on the Richter scale, making it the most powerful earthquake ever recorded! An earthquake at 9.5 is 10 million times stronger than one at 2.5.

Not only did this quake affect Chile, but a massive wave ran through the Pacific Ocean. It created a tsunami which had enough force to travel over 9,321 miles, causing death and destruction in Hawaii and Japan. Luckily, the people of Chile knew that trouble was coming. A series of warning quakes had been hitting the area, so people had time to evacuate.

In this case, it wasn't the number of lives lost or damage to buildings, but the amount of energy released from beneath Earth's surface that makes this #4 on our list!

EARTHQUAKE IN CHILE

A man prays among the ruins of his house in Valdivia.

WHAT HAPPENED?

The epicenter of the earthquake was around 197 feet down below the Pacific Ocean floor and about 99 miles off the coast of Chile. The closest towns of Valdivia and Puerto Montt suffered the greatest damage.

WHAT'S THE DAMAGE?

The earthquake caused landslides that were so enormous they changed the course of major rivers or dammed them up, creating new lakes. The land along the coast of Chile, particularly in the port city of Puerto Montt, sank. Over 125,000 homes were completely destroyed, totaling over $185 million in losses. Other damages included over $65 million to agriculture and more than $30 million to industry and trade.

epicenter: *part of Earth's surface directly above an earthquake*

? With so much loss in agriculture, industry, and trade, how does this affect the surrounding areas?

CASUALTIES

Lives lost: 2,000
Injured/affected: 3,000 people injured and two million left homeless in Chile

PICKING UP THE PIECES

Foreign countries including Germany, Argentina, and Sweden lent a helping hand through foreign aid. The largest contributions came from the United States with donations and loans totaling over $30 million.

? Besides cash, what other forms of aid can other countries contribute?

Quick Fact

The Chilean town of Quenuir has a saying, "The tsunami was so big that it even took the dead from their graves." This is because several coffins were unearthed and washed away in the tsunami caused by the 1960 quake.

THE BIG ONES

Just because an earthquake is the most powerful doesn't mean it's also the deadliest. Check out this fact chart with the five most intense earthquakes, and compare them with the five deadliest earthquakes.

5 LARGEST EARTHQUAKES IN TERMS OF MAGNITUDE SINCE 1900

LOCATION	DATE	MAGNITUDE
Chile	May 22, 1960	9.5
Prince William Sound, Alaska	March 28, 1964	9.2
Andreanof Islands, Aleutian Islands	March 9, 1957	9.1
Kamchatka, Soviet Union	November 4, 1962	9.0
Sumatra, Indonesia	December 26, 2004	9.0

5 LARGEST EARTHQUAKES IN TERMS OF FATALITIES

LOCATION	DATE	MAGNITUDE	DEATHS
Tangshan, China	July 27, 1976	7.5	300,000
Sumatra, Indonesia	December 26, 2004	9.0	255,000
Tsinghai, China	May 22, 1927	7.9	200,000
Gansu, China	December 16, 1920	7.8	200,000
Kwanto, Japan	September 1, 1923	7.9	143,000

The Expert Says...

"At the moment the earthquake hit, we had trouble walking. ... I walked downtown because the university is really close to the sea and we were afraid a tsunami would follow."

— Survivor Santiago Fernandez from Arica, Chile

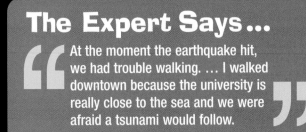

Take Note

Although the 1960 earthquake in Chile caused fewer deaths than some of the other disasters in this book, it is still the biggest earthquake to date. Countless buildings and homes were destroyed, land was permanently changed, and new records were set by this disaster. For these reasons, we ranked this natural disaster #4.

• Why is it important to have an evacuation plan in case of a natural disaster? What is needed for an evacuation to go smoothly?

This satellite image shows the coastline of Kalutara, Sri Lanka, taken December 26, 2004, shortly after the impact of the tsunami. Notice how close the houses are to the coastline.

2004

PLACE: Coasts of South and East Asia and as far away as Eastern Africa

WHEN: December 26, 2004

LEVEL OF DESTRUCTION: This catastrophe wreaked havoc across two continents! Almost 300,000 people were killed and millions were left homeless.

On December 26, 2004, a massive earthquake measuring over 9.0 on the Richter scale struck under the sea near the northern Indonesian island of Sumatra. This was the fifth biggest earthquake ever recorded.

The energy released from this giant earthquake caused the displacement of tons of water. Massive tsunamis, Japanese for harbor waves, came crashing into the shores of many countries in the South Indian Ocean. These waves destroyed many islands, killing over 200,000 people.

This natural disaster is ranked #3 on our list because of the amount of energy released from the earth, and the damage and destruction it caused.

tsunamis: *long high sea waves caused by underwater earthquakes or other disturbances*

TSUNAMI OF 2004

WHAT HAPPENED?

Waves as high as 98 feet hit Sumatra, followed by Thailand, India, Sri Lanka, Malaysia, Somalia, and many other countries. Within seven hours of the first wave hitting, the tsunami reached the eastern coast of Africa almost 3,728 miles away.

WHAT'S THE DAMAGE?

These deadly waves smashed down buildings and destroyed properties several hundred feet inland. When the waves retreated, they dragged everything, including people, into the sea. Many drowned and others were killed when they became entangled in deadly debris. Many coastal resorts were destroyed.

Quick Fact

The earthquake that caused the tsunami was so strong that the entire rotation of Earth was affected. On December 26, 2004, the day was a few microseconds shorter than it should have been!

CASUALTIES

Lives lost: Almost 300,000
Injured/affected: Five million people were displaced from their homes.

PICKING UP THE PIECES

Money for relief poured in from all over the world for this disaster. Schools and businesses started fundraising almost immediately. The largest donations were from Australia with $815 million, followed by Germany with $660 million, and Japan with $500 million.

? Large bodies of water produce tsunamis and hurricanes, two dangerous forces of nature. Knowing this, would you want to live by water? Why or why not?

Women grieve as they pass by boats destroyed by the tsunami in the southern Indian state of Tamil Nadu.

Quick Fact

According to the U.S. Geological Survey, the 2004 tsunami is estimated to have released the energy of 23,000 atomic bombs.

The Expert Says...

" The world's worst tsunami was the one [December 26] 2004, off Sumatra, killing more than 200,000 people. The triggering quake was the largest the Earth has experienced in 40 years. "

— Professor Andrew Miall, Department of Geology, University of Toronto, Canada

WAVE OF HORROR

The tsunami of 2004 will be remembered by everyone for a long time to come. The loss of human life was staggering. These quotes reveal some of the heartbreaking facts and stories ...

JAN EGELAND, A UNITED NATIONS EMERGENCY RELIEF COORDINATOR:
"The problem with tsunamis is that it takes hours — or minutes — for this wall of water to come, and there's just very, very little time."

U.S. PRESIDENT GEORGE W. BUSH:
"On this first day of a new year, we join the world in feeling enormous sadness over a great human tragedy. ... The carnage is of a scale that defies comprehension."

carnage: *bloodshed*

SIMON CLARK, LONDON, VACATIONING IN KOH NGAI, THAILAND:
"People that were snorkeling were dragged along the coral and washed up on the beach, and people that were sunbathing got washed into the sea."

MODEL PETRA NEMCOVA, VACATIONING IN THAILAND, WHO LOST HER BOYFRIEND:
"People were screaming and kids were screaming all over the place, screaming, 'Help, help.' And after a few minutes you didn't hear the kids anymore."

SUE RUSSELL WHO LIVES ON THE ISLAND OF PHUKET:
"And thousands of people don't know where their loved ones are. They are just walking around trying to find them."

Take Note

The destructive force behind this natural disaster killed hundreds of thousands of people across two continents. The survivors were displaced from their homes. Many tourists died or lost loved ones. This international disaster ranks #3 on our list.
• Much of this disaster was caught on video by tourists who reached safety in time. Would you like to see graphic footage of this destructive tsunami? Explain why or why not.

5   4   **3**   2   1

The Sahel drought shattered the economy, reduced water supplies, and contributed to the starvation of hundreds of thousands of people.

MALNOURISHED BOY—GETTY IMAGES/REPORTAGE/PER-ANDERSPETTERSSON

HEL REGION, AFRICA

PLACE: The Sahel region of Africa, which includes almost a dozen countries

WHEN: Late 1960s through the 1980s, and in some parts of Africa today

LEVEL OF DESTRUCTION: Fertile soil turned into desert-like land, causing over a million people to starve to death.

Clear and sunny skies seem like a great weather forecast, but what if it stayed that way for decades with no rain? Even for the Sahel region of Africa, which is accustomed to dry weather, extended periods without rain can be devastating. And when little or no rain fell in the region for two decades from the late 1960s to the 1980s, it was a disaster. This problem still exists today.

Droughts are long periods of time when there is little to no rainfall. Why would dry weather lead to a disaster? Imagine how all the things around you need rain and water to survive. Flowers, crops, and animals need their fill of H_2O. And don't forget about people. How would a week without water affect the environment? How about a year? Try over 20 years! Without water, crops won't grow, animals will die, rivers and lakes will dry up, and people will starve to death.

A high death toll and major changes to the environment place this disaster at #2 on our list.

DROUGHT IN SAHEL REGION, AFRICA

WHAT HAPPENED?

This drought led to a massive famine that still exists today. Lakes dried up, farmland was destroyed, and millions of livestock died. This was disastrous for the economy because agriculture is very important to the nations in this region. About 70 percent of African workers were employed in the farming industry.

WHAT'S THE DAMAGE?

The Sahel region borders the Sahara desert, and the drought caused the desert to spread southward into this region. Five countries (Ethiopia, Sudan, Mali, Niger, and Chad) were among the worst hit. Those able to survive were forced to move to areas that were already crowded.

CASUALTIES

Lives lost: More than one million
Injured/affected: More than 50 million people have been displaced.

PICKING UP THE PIECES

There has been an ongoing relief effort to help the people of the Sahel region. The main goal is to aid in the development of these areas instead of fighting the drought. The United Nations and the Red Cross have helped out for decades. Many countries also donate money, equipment, and supplies.

? What other relief organizations have donated money to help victims of natural disasters? Give specific examples using researched information.

? What would be the challenges of living in the desert?

Quick Fact

In 1984, Irish musician Bob Geldof founded a charity called Band Aid to raise money for the food crisis in Ethiopia. He called up a bunch of his friends in music, and they recorded the song *Do They Know It's Christmas?* A few of the many artists who participated were Sting, Bono, David Bowie, and Paul McCartney.

Relief workers distribute food to hungry people.

The Expert Says...

" Not every natural hazard has to turn into a natural disaster. Good policies and good scientific research can help to reduce the impacts on society and the environment of natural hazards such as severe prolonged drought. "

— Michael H. Glantz, director, National Center for Atmospheric Research

THE FOOD CRISIS IN NIGER

A Web article from *National Black Catholic Congress*
By Kimberly Mazyck

Recent news stories have alerted the world about the severe food scarcity in the Sahel region of Africa, especially in Niger … Most of the affected regions are extremely poor.

Even in a normal year, it is hard to grow a crop that can feed families adequately. In the summer of 2004, there was a plague of locusts in the Sahelian region of Western Africa. According to the World Food Programme, this was the worst locust plague to hit the Sahel region in 15 years. Massive swarms of billions of hungry locusts ate their way across much of West Africa. The swarms destroyed thousands of acres of crops such as corn, millet, and sorghum just before they were due to be harvested. The locusts ruined fields and farms across a vast stretch of Mali, Mauritania, and Senegal …

As a result, a serious food shortage is affecting more than 3.6 million people in Niger alone. The locusts and the drought virtually destroyed food production across the predominantly agricultural country. Catholic Relief Services (CRS) estimates that as many as 3,815 villages have lost 50 percent or more of their food production. People are eating leaves and grass, selling personal items, removing their children from school, and migrating to neighboring cities and countries to find work or food …

locusts: *type of grasshopper that can devastate crops within minutes*

Quick Fact

At first, scientists thought human activity (such as deforestation for farming) had changed the climate enough to cause the Sahel drought. In 2003, researchers discovered that the drought could have been caused by a change in ocean temperature. When the oceans around Africa are just a bit warmer than average, the rainfall stays over the ocean and doesn't move toward land.

Take Note

With more than a million dead and some 50 million affected, no disaster on this list has matched the devastation of this drought. The fact that the Sahel region continues to suffer decades later makes this the second-largest disaster in history.

• This drought has been going on for so long that even our media no longer regard the troubles of the Sahel victims as newsworthy. What would you like to see done for the people of the Sahel region? How would you raise awareness and money?

5   4   3   **2**   1

The 3,395-mile-long Yellow River has been responsible for many of China's worst floods.

ER FLOOD, CHINA

PLACE: Yellow River, also known as Huang He, China

WHEN: Summer of 1931

LEVEL OF DESTRUCTION: Millions of people dead and over 38,610 square miles of land destroyed

Water is important to life and industry, which is why people choose to live near rivers. In China, millions have settled along the banks of one of its longest rivers, the Yellow River. The water is crucial for personal use, farming, industrial purposes, and transportation. The river's name comes from the large amount of silt that makes it look yellow. The Yellow River is also known as "China's Sorrow" because over the centuries it has killed more people than any other river. The worst flood in the 20th century occurred in the summer of 1931.

What made this flood so disastrous? Entire villages were washed away, and many people drowned. When the water failed to drain away in time, crops were totally destroyed, and it was too late to replant. People were not only weakened by starvation, but they also contracted diseases from the contaminated water, causing a health epidemic that killed even more.

Read on to find out why this disaster comes in at the #1 spot on our list.

silt: *fine soil*

YELLOW RIVER FLOOD, CHINA

WHAT HAPPENED?

Heavy rains caused most of the levees to break and give way, resulting in the flooding of the Yellow River. In some areas the water was almost 10 feet deep. This flood caused crops to wash away, depriving the people who inhabited the area around the Yellow River of food. In addition, water became contaminated and people fell sick with malaria and other diseases.

WHAT'S THE DAMAGE?

It is estimated that over 43,630 square miles of China were flooded — that's about the size of New York State! The land and soil were utterly ruined, and millions of people were forced to move since their homes were destroyed.

> **?** The Yellow River has a scary history of constant floods. Why do you think people keep moving back to the banks of the river?

Quick Fact

The Yellow River is over 3,107 miles long. It begins high above sea level in the northern mountain province and ends at the Yellow Sea.

CASUALTIES

Lives lost: Approximately 3.5 million (the number is so huge that an exact figure is not known)

Injured/affected: Millions were made homeless.

PICKING UP THE PIECES

Apparently, enough dams and levees could possibly stop this raging river from overflowing, but that would require a lot of money and human resources. So for now, the people in China are attempting to build more levees and are keeping their fingers crossed that it will be at least another 100 years before the Yellow River floods again. However, the Chinese are definitely not counting on nature's goodwill. Many major dams, levees, and flood control projects are underway.

Quick Fact

The Yellow River has changed course many times, due to dams, levees, wars, and rainfall.

The Expert Says...

"A very tragic example [of flooding] occurred when the Yellow and Yangtze Rivers in China flooded, resulting in 3.7 million fatalities, some directly from drowning and many from the disease and crop failures that resulted."

— Matt Kelsch, meteorologist, University Corporation for Atmospheric Research

The Yellow River runs through nine provinces and provides water for 12 percent of China's population.

China's Sorrow

So you're probably wondering — why is the Yellow River so deadly? This article and fact chart describe why this river keeps flooding and the damage it's done in the last 150 years.

This river is full of loose material called loess [low-ess], which is blown in from the Gobi Desert. Although loess provides fertile soil for farming, heavy rains wash the loess into the water, loading the Yellow River with sediment. There comes a point where the river flattens out and slows down. At this point, most of the sediment settles in the riverbed, and the river is raised a few inches every year. Although the people try to build levees along the riverbanks, they can't keep up with the rising river. This means the levees are being built higher and higher. As the centuries passed, the river began rising above the surrounding land, and so the levees did too. In some parts of the Yellow River, the water stands as much as 33 feet above the land.

Chinese residents try to wade past flood waters in search of high ground in 2005.

YEAR: 1887
DEATH TOLL: Between 900,000 and six million
SAD FACT: This was the worst natural disaster recorded in history until 1931.

YEAR: 1938
DEATH TOLL: 900,000
SAD FACT: Chinese soldiers intentionally broke the levees to keep Japanese soldiers from invading.

YEAR: 1943
DEATH TOLL: Three million
SAD FACT: This flood destroyed crops and caused most of these people to starve.

Take Note

Throughout history, floods have proven to be the deadliest natural disasters. This is mainly due to the large number of people who live by water. This disaster caused the highest number of deaths on our list and caused extensive damage to the surrounding land. That's why we placed this natural disaster at #1 on our list.

• This flood caused millions of people to die, not just from the actual flood but all of the secondary effects afterward. What do you think could have been done to prevent so many people from losing their lives?

5   **4**   **3**   **2**   **1**

We Thought …

Here are the criteria we used in ranking the 10 worst natural disasters.

The disaster:
- Caused a significant number of fatalities
- Caused severe damage to property, business, and crops
- Devastated a large area
- Lasted for a considerable length of time
- Was unpredictable
- Hit highly populated areas
- Affected a large population
- Required a massive relief effort and expensive cleanup

What Do You Think?

1. Do you agree with our ranking? If you don't, try ranking them yourself. Justify your ranking with data from your own research and reasoning. You may refer to our criteria, or you may want to draw up your own list of criteria.

2. Here are three other natural disasters that we considered but in the end did not include in our top 10 list: the Exxon Valdez spill; the hurricane in Bangladesh, 1970; and the landslide in Gansu, China, 1920.
   - Find out more about them. Do you think they should have made our list? Give reasons for your response.
   - Are there other natural disasters that you think should have made our list? Explain your choices.

Index